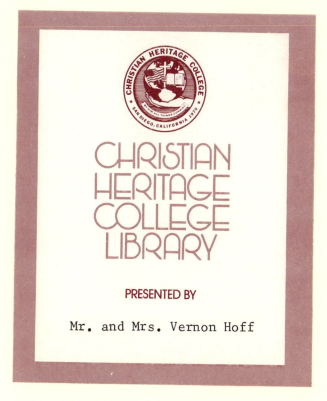

PAUL VERLAINE
Poems

TRANSLATOR · JACQUES LECLERCQ

ILLUSTRATIONS · STANLEY WYATT

GREENWOOD PRESS, PUBLISHERS
WESTPORT, CONNECTICUT

Library of Congress Cataloging in Publication Data

Verlaine, Paul Marie, 1844-1896.
    Poems.

    Reprint of the ed. published by Peter Pauper
Press, Mount Vernon, N. Y.
    I.   Le Clercq, Jacques Georges Clemenceau, 1898-
1972.
PQ2463.A25   1977   841'.8   77-13574
ISBN 0-8371-9859-3

FOR TANAQUIL

The Verlaine of her Childhood

Reprinted in 1977 by Greenwood Press, Inc.
51 Riverside Avenue, Westport, CT. 06880

Printed in the United States of America

FOREWORD

PAUL VERLAINE *(1844–1896) has exerted a fabulous influence because of the sincerity, the simplicity, the symbolism, the poignancy, the musicality and the impressionistic vagueness in his verse. Childlike in vice or virtue, he lived a life that was in turn pure, placid, bland and touching; or evil, stormy, tragic and revolting. Its landmarks are early association with famed poets, his first book in 1866, his marriage in 1870, his growing alcoholism, and his abandonment of his bride in 1871 in favor of vagabonding with Rimbaud. When Rimbaud sought to abandon* him, *Verlaine fired a revolver that cost him two years in Belgium jails. Here the renegade returned to Christianity, a sincere but unpersevering convert. His wife divorced him in 1875.*

In 1881, Sagesse, *a book of highly emotional religious verse, brought him fame and authority. He undertook schoolmastering in England and France, then made a fiasco of the farm he had bought and where he lived with his "adoptive" son, Létinois. Thereafter, save for a brief visit to lecture at Oxford, the rest of his life was spent in prolonged commuting trips between saloons and hospital wards.*

Countless authors have depicted him; I mention only France who put him into a novel, George Moore who swears he found him sober, and, in our day, Compton Mackenzie. Musicians, mostly, interpreted him best; I cite Debussy, Fauré, Hahn, Louis Ganne, Massager and Ravel — but there are more.

At several conservatories, students of composition are obliged to set Verlaine to music.

He is easier to put into music than into words: untranslatable into a foreign tongue, he yet remains and will ever remain a challenge to translators, including this one. I have selected for translation a representative spread of Verlaine's many kinds of poems, making a kind of sampler rather than a parade of what in the originals are his best.

These poems present him as a would-be objectivist, sculptured and plastic; as a delicate painter of Watteauesque pastels; as a starry-eyed lover; as a repentant Christian with egregious lapses; as the victim of an immature half-hope and half-despair; as a crapulous lecher with promiscuous perversions; and in French at least as a tunesmith of the highest order.

In an essay, Anatole France stated: "You cannot judge him as you would a rational man . . . he is at once much more and much less than we . . . he is crazy, you say, and I agree with you heartily! But take care lest they tell of him, as they tell of Villon, that he was the noblest poet of his age!" I quote this only to show the impact of Verlaine upon a highly skeptical and discriminating mind. Think then of his effect on all the Romantics, the Parnassians, and — especially — the Symbolists, Rimbaud and Mallarmé!

JACQUES LE CLERCQ

POEMS · VERLAINE

TO ARTHUR RIMBAUD

MORTAL, angel and demon — as well say Rimbaud! —
In this my book yours is the first and foremost place,
Though some crazed scribbler wrote you down an
    embryo
Monster, a beardless rake, a crapulous disgrace.
Spirals of incense smoke and gold chords from the lyre
Acclaim your entrance in the halls of memory,
Because you loved me even as such love should be
Your name shall be writ gloriously in signs of fire.

Women will prize your height and strength with bated
    breath
And the young proud allure of your rustic sly bearing,
Very desirable you are, languid yet daring;
History sculptured you triumphant over death
And savoring life's joys to the purest excesses —
Your white feet poised, indifferent, on Envy's tresses.

TO MY SON GEORGES

As Ovid's book sped so this book of mine shall speed
    From exile to the city.
Rome banished him; I, by a more perfidious deed,
    Am banished without pity

Far from my son! Shall I see you? I, dead or no,
    Here is my Will: *"Adore*
God; hate no man alive; bear your name even so
    As they who went before."

SAPPHO

Furious, her breasts stiffening, her eyes hollow and sore,
Sappho tormented by the pricks of her desire,
Runs like a famished wolf along the icy shore . . .
Forgetful of the Rite, she thinks of Phaon. Afire
With spite and wrath for her tears scorned, in mute despair
She tears out handfuls of her massive tangled hair.

Then, through her measureless remorse, Time in his sweep
Evokes the days when pure, radiant and glorying
In love she fashioned songs the heart's remembering
Echoes in the black night to virgins as they sleep.
Now Sappho shuts her eyes. Silence. A frantic leap
Into the grey-black sea that rises, welcoming,
As pale Selene, friend of Tribads, in one swing,
Bursts, vengeful, through the heavens to calcinate the
    deep.

PUPPETS

Pulcinella and Scaramouch
Black on the moon, plotting, I vouch,
Make violent gestures as they pass.
Meanwhile the good Bologna doctor
Saunters observantly to proctor
The fields for simples in the grass.
His daughter then — a pawky face! —
Slips through the arbor with sly grace,
Half-nude and soundless on the trail
Of her adored Spanish corsair
Whose sharp distress pierces the air
Voiced by the languid nightingale.

8

AFTER THREE YEARS

I pushed the tottering door. In a lost hour
I paced the little garden where a pane
Of morning sunlight shining on the lane
Wove spangles of moist sparks for every flower.
Nothing is changed; I saw the humble bower
With its wild vines and chairs of rattan cane,
The fountain still sobbed silvery songs in vain,
The aspen moaned eternally and our,

Our own red roses throbbed; and ecstasies
Of tall proud lilies fluttered in the breeze.
I recognized each swallow as it flew,
I found the statued nymph with its regrets
For chips and scales strewn on the avenue —
Slim, with stale scents of weeds and mignonettes. . . .

PARISIAN LANDSCAPE

Moonlight laid down her shining tints of zinc
        At wide obtuse angles,
Thick smokeclouds, shaped like 5's, adorned the brink
Of the tall pointed roofs with blue-black spangles.

The wind wept through the grey sky's solitude,
        Deep, like a bassoon.
Far off, a cat, discreet and chilly, mewed
In shrill and curious fashion at the moon.

Strolling I dreamed of Plato; on and on,
        My thoughts, a dense mass,
Ranged over Salamis and Marathon,
Under blue lamp-posts twinkling eyes of gas. . . .

10

WEARINESS

O gentleness and gentleness and gentleness!
Calm these mad febrile fits of passion; be discreet;
For sometimes woman in the fire of pleasure's heat
Should show a sisterlike peaceful submissiveness.
Be languorous, lavish your halcyon caress
In placid sighs and in shy glances that retreat —
Jealous embraces and obsessive spasms, sweet,
Are not worth one long kiss — even in faithlessness. . . .

But in your golden heart, you say, child, as you pant,
That savage passions rise, sounding the olifant?
So let the trollop trumpet in unhindered play!
Rest your brow on my brow, clasp my hand in your hand,
Pledge me bright vows tomorrow must needs countermand,
And, O hot-blooded sweetheart, let me weep till day!

THE SHEPHERD'S HOUR

Aloft the moon is red in the dense smoke
Of mists that dance over the slumbering
Vaporous meadowland; a quivering
Sways the green rushes where the grey frogs croak.

Petals of waterflowers fold for the night;
Far off, tall serried poplars stand outlined
Like shadowy grey specters, ill-defined . . .
The fireflies prick the brakes with dots of light. . . .

The screech owls waken but you cannot hear
Their heavy oar-like wings row through the air,
The zenith fills with muffled light — and there:
White — Venus looms at last — and night is here.

11

THE GENTLE SONG

Hear the soft song, all down and gloss,
Which weeps for only your delight,
It is discreet and it is light:
Tremors of water over moss.

That voice once known to you (and dear?)
Is veiled at present and its fate
Is, like a widow's, desolate
Yet proud withal and free from fear.

Deep in her long veil's folds it trembles
In autumn breezes, near or far,
And for the startled heart dissembles
To manifest truth like a star.

It tells with faint familiar hum
How kindliness is all our life
And how from hate, envy and strife
Nothing remains when death is come.

It tells how glorious to be
Simple, waiting for nothing here,
It sings gold weddings and sincere
Joy in peace without victory.

Welcome the low persistent voice
In its ingenuous wedding song.
Ah, what makes souls more blithe and strong
Than to help other souls rejoice?

How "transient" and "at a loss,"
That soul which suffers without wrath,
And yet how clear its sense and path!
Hear the soft song, all down and gloss.

12

CLAIR DE LUNE

Your soul is a choice countryside astir
With charming lovers masked in graceful guises,
Dancing and playing lutes and, as it were,
Half-sad under their curious disguises.
So, as they sing, always in minor key,
Of Love (how brave!) and Life (how opportune!)
They seem to doubt their own felicity,
While their blithe song blends with the pallid moon
In calm clear light that only sad skies capture,
Making the nesting birds dream as it mounts,
As the tall jets of water sob with rapture,
The tall svelte jets rising from marble founts.

TWILIGHT

The sunset darted its last crimson bars
As the wind cradled the pale nenuphars . . .
The giant nenuphars by reed and rush
Gleamed, sad, on waters in the twilight hush . . .
I wandered, lone, baring my wound beside
The pond, among the willows, where a wide
Vague mist evoked in the still evening air
A tall and milky phantom in despair
And weeping with the voice of teals who beat
Their wings, calling upon their hosts to meet
Among the willows where I wandered, lone,
Baring my wound; and the shroud of thick-sewn
Shadows bore down to drown the long last rays
Of sunset over the pale waters; and always
Tall nenuphars, swaying by reed and rush —
Nenuphars shining in the twilight hush. . . .

13

GROTESQUES

Their own legs are their only nags,
Their only gold lies in their gaze,
Haggard they go, and clad in rags,
Venturesome down venturous ways.

Shocked sages rant with righteous phlegm,
Fools pity these mad gamblers, dear
Children stick out their tongues at them,
Harridans gape at them and sneer.

Because, ridiculous and lush
And odious in the extreme,
Their figures seen against the dusk
Are phantoms from an evil dream.

Because each on his shrill guitar,
Clenching the hand of liberty,
Snuffles out songs that ring bizarre,
Nostalgic and refractory,

Because — fastidious — in their eyes
Loved things, perpetual and deep
(Old dead and ancient deities)
Rise suddenly to laugh and weep. . . .

Go, vagabonds, go evermore,
Stray, baleful and accursèd thrice,
Along abyss and ditch and shore
Under a purblind Paradise . . .

Nature and mankind are allied
Duly to crush that disrespect,
That melancholy, and that pride,
Which make you stride with head erect;

In you they punish blasphemy
Of hopes, vasty and vehement,
They bruise your damned heads furiously
With every butting element.

Torrid Junes burn and raw Decembers
Freeze your flesh to the very bones
As fevers roast your aching members,
Wounded by thorns and maimed by stones.

All things repulse you, all things hurt,
So when Death dawns to bring you ease,
Your corpses — a chill moldering dirt —
Even the wolves will scoff at these!

A SONG OF AUTUMN

The fiddles long
  Sob out their song
    Of autumn's moan,
      Wounding my heart
      With languid art
      In monotone.
Choking and pale
  When without fail
    The hour tolls deep,
      I think at last
      Of old days past
      And I weep . . .
And I go hence
  In the violence
    Of the wind's grief,
      Hither and yon,
      Ever anon
      Like a dead leaf.

THE BOURGEOIS

Monsieur Philistine, district mayor and family head,
Is grave; his collar swallows up his ears; his eyes
Float, careless in an endless dream of vague surmise.
Spring blooms upon his bedroom slippers. He is dead
To wizardry of moonlight and to magic shed
On shady graves where birds sing to the glistening skies,
To lush fields and far hills where the lark's last note dies.
Monsieur Philistine muses of his girl to wed

To Monsieur Thingummy, a youthful, wealthy, staunch
Prosaic botanist with a decided paunch;
As for scribblers of verse, those worthless absinthe-sippers,
Those bearded ne'er-do-wells, those futile rogues, he holds
Them in a deeper horror than his endless colds . . .
And Spring in flower blossoms on his bedroom slippers.

PANTOMIME

Pierrot — not a Clitander, he! —
Empties a flagon jauntily,
Then downs a pie. (Man must be fed!)
Cassandra strolls the garden, wan,
Shedding salt unknown tears upon
Her nephew, disinherited!
That ruffian Harlequin designs
A sly abduction — Columbine's . . .
He pirouettes four times with art:
Columbine dreams in strange new ease
Feeling strange pricklings in the breeze
And hearing voices fill her heart.

LUCIEN LÉTINOIS

Since my *own* son was stolen from my keeping,
To have adopted you for my own child
Was not of Heaven's counsel. Mad or mild,
Often I said this to my true self. Weeping,

Always I said this as I eyed your tomb,
Half charcoal-black, half-white with marguerites . . .
Surely here was one of those shabby feats
Which wreak the present sorrows of my doom.

It was, I fear, a flaw in reasoning.
All things considered, I had no just right
To find rapt consolation in my plight
And choose you — howsoever bland the thing! —

For even our meek plan of hidden action
In virtue — land, a cottage without taste
Known of the poor — and for a joy (how chaste!)
God's grace in its protective satisfaction.

I should have left you in your poor blithe nest,
I should have spared you my too stormy passion,
I should have served my exile in proud fashion
Far from my *own* son born of rites thrice-blest.

Reaching the heyday of maturity,
A man, he would have sought me out, to sense
Knowing how crushed his father was, how tense
A victim to evil stupidity!

So this adoption was forbidden fruit,
It should have passed the scent and coolness of
The tree and fruit, indifferent to love . . .
Thus Heaven punishes the dissolute!

18

IN THE WOODS

Some — I mean innocents or whose lymphs turned too
    drear —
Find forest spells merely languid and indolent:
Cool breezes and warm fragrances! They are content!
But others — dreamers, they — feel seized with mystic fear.

They are content! But I, nervous, crazed by a dread
Fearsome and vague remorse from noon to bitter noon,
I tremble in the forest like some dazed poltroon
Who funks an ambush or has looked upon the dead.

These great boughs that can never be appeased — a wave
Whence a black silence falls from shadows blacker still —
This whole grim sinister décor cannot but fill
My spirit with a horror, trivial, deep and grave.

Chiefly on summer twilights when in the red sky
Sunsets blend with the greyish blue of vaporous
Mists that they tint with flame and blood; the angelus,
Tinkling far off, sounds like a plaintive nearing cry.

The wind soars, warm and heavy; tremors pass apace
And pass and pass again across the densities
Of the high ever-darkening oaks; obsessive, these
Shudderings scatter, like miasmas, over space.

Night falls. The owl flies off. Now comes the time when we
Recall naïve old wives' tales on dead evenings . . .
Yonder, yonder beneath a thicket the live springs
Breed sounds like hidden footpads plotting murderously.

KLASSISCHE WALPURGISNACHT

Here is a Faustian sabbath (not Part One, Part Two)
A rhythmic sabbath, verily rhythmic, extremely
Rhythmic. Picture a garden by Lenôtre, too
    Charming, ridiculous and seemly.

Fountains centered in circuses, and lanes that head
Dead forward; marble sylvans; by way of marines,
Bronze sea gods; here and there a Venus, spread;
    Trim quincunxes and bowling greens.

Tall chestnut trees; patches of flowers forming the dune,
Here, of dwarf rose trees, laid out tastefully, and spiss;
Further along, yews trimmed in triangles . . . the moon
    Of summer nights over all this.

Midnight tolls. Deep in the old park, it wakes the low
Notes of a melancholy hunting song that stir
Gently from the soft horns, muffled and slow,
    The view halloo from *Tannhaüser*.

Veiled airs from far-off horns in which the tenderness
Of all the senses grasps the frightened heart in strains
Tunefully dissonant in their rapt happiness,
    As, at the call of their refrains,

Sudden translucent figures that lye moonlight blanches
Meld in a close embrace and interwoven go
Opaline through the greenish shadows of the branches:
    Raffet's dream-sketch of a Watteau!

They intertwine under the virid shade of trees
With languid gestures — is not their despair profound? —
Then all about the shrubs, marbles and bronzes, these
    Figures dance slowly in a round.

These restive specters, can they be the poet's proud
And drunken thoughts or his remorse or tears he shed?
(These restive specters whirling in an eerie cadenced
    crowd)
    Or, very simply, are they dead?

O dreamer, wooed by horror, tell me, yes or no,
Are these your thoughts, remorse or tears? — Eh? —
    good or bad?
(These specters whirled by a resistless vertigo!)
    Or dead men who might well be mad?

No matter! On they go, a feverish spectral band,
Bouncing in their vast dance, mournful and desolate,
As in rays of the atom's sunshine, here they stand,
    Then suddenly disintegrate.

Humid and pallid when Dawn rises, whitely stark,
To hush each horn in turn, so that at length, supremely,
Nothing is left — supremely — just Lenôtre's park,
    Charming, ridiculous and seemly.

NOCTURNAL

Night. Rain. A pale sky pinked out by a set
Of spires and openwork towers. . . . The silhouette
Of an extinguished Gothic city in the grey
Distance...the plain...a gallows where the victims sway,
Scraggy, pecked by the avid beaks of crows, and where
They dance nonpareil jigs upon the sable air,
Their feet rich pasture for the wolves. A few

Sparse thornbushes, and here and there, holly or yew
Rear all the horror of their foliage, left and right,
On the fuliginous, jumbled *décor* of night,
Rough-sketched. And then three prisoners, as though
    ranged in tiers,
Livid and barefoot, flanked by mighty halberdiers,
Marching; their blades, straight as are harrow blades,
    shine plain
Counterwise to the lances of the falling rain.

IL BACIO

O kiss, — hollyhock in the garden of a rapt caress!
On the teeth's keyboard a lively accompaniment
Of soft refrains Love sings in hearts lost and intent
With his archangel voice in witching languidness.

O graceful kiss, O kiss resonant and divine,
O matchless ecstasy, delight too sweet to cloy,
Hail! . . . Man, bending above your heady cup of joy
Grows drunken with the fruit of your exhaustless vine.

Like Rhine wine and like music — lavish in your ways —
Solace you bring. All grief expires before your gold
Together with the pout in your purpurine fold . . .
Goethe and Will alone can hymn your classic praise.

I — a mere wretched Paris troubadour — meanwhile
Can bring out this bouquet of childish verses duly . . .
But, kindly and for prize: descend on the unruly
Lips of One I adore, O Kiss, descend and smile.

MY FAMILIAR DREAM

This strange familiar dream oft haunts my sleeping:
A woman unknown I love — and who loves *me!*
Who never looks alike nor differently,
And, understanding, holds my heart in keeping.
She and she only understands me, sweeping
Doubt from my heart; she only sets me free
From problems that beset me; only she
Freshens my pale brow's fever with her weeping.

Is her hair fair or dark or red? Who knows?
Her name? It bears a blessed lilt like those
Of loved ones whom Life banished as it willed.
Her glance is like the glance of statues; as
For her calm, grave and distant voice, it has
The accent of dear voices that are stilled.

PROSPECT

So it shall be on a clear summer day,
The sun, accomplice of my joy and peace,
Shining on silks and satins shall increase
Your loved sweet charms in every witching way.

The sky, blue as a tent, tapering and tense,
Shall shudder, sumptuous, in long folds upon
Our two so joyous brows as they turn wan
For our deep happiness and this suspense,

And when comes evening, the melodious air
Shall play, caressing, in your veils. Afar
The peaceful gleam of each and every star
Shall smile benignly on the bridal pair.

SENTIMENTAL DIALOGUE

Through the old park, lonely and frozen fast,
A moment since, two darksome figures passed.

Their lips how flabby, and their eyes how dead!
And who has overheard the words they said?

In the old park, lonely and frozen fast,
Two revenants just now evoked the past.

"Do you recall our ancient ecstasy?" —
"Ought I do so? What can it mean to me?"

*"Does my mere name still fire your spirit so
That through your dreams you always see me?"* — *"No!"*

*"Ah, the sweet days of happiness when we
Hung lip to lip in rapture."* — *"That may be!"*

"How blue the heavens were, our hopes how high!" ...
"Hope, vanquished, fled across a murky sky."

Through the wild oatfields thus these phantoms sped
Black Night alone could hear the words they said.

THE FAUN

An ancient terra cotta faun
    Grins at us from the bowling green,
        Presaging evils that must dawn
            Too surely on days too serene

That led you and led me aright,
    Sorrowful pilgrims in our labors
        Up to this very hour whose flight
            Spins to the blatant roll of tabors.

NOCTURNE

Bright moonrays blanch
The woodland trees,
From every branch
Soar melodies,
Below, above —
O Love, my love!

This pond ashine,
White as a pillow,
Reflects the line
Of one lone willow
Where the winds weep —
Dream we now deep!

Peacefulness, come
Of rapt content
Sinks slowly from
The firmament
Like a moonflower —
Now is Love's hour!

OBLIVION

Vast black slumber falls deep
On my life which expires —
All hopes, go to sleep,
Go to sleep, all desires.

I see nothing; Night fills
Me; remembrances fail
Of past good and past ills.
O the poor sorry tale!

I a cradle in gloom
That a hand seems to brush
In the depths of a tomb:
Silence, hush! . . .

DAWN

Before you vanish, pale
Star of sweet morning-time
    — Myriad quail
Sing, sing amid the thyme —

Turn toward the poet, mark
How bright with love his eyes
    — Now the lark
Soars to the wakening skies —

Turn your glance ere dawn's light
Drown it in blue defeat
    —What delight
Fills the fields of ripe wheat! —

Then make my thought gleam through
Yonder, far, far away
    — See the dew
Shine gaily on the hay —

To where dreams, slumber's gift,
Charm my belovèd one
    — Swift, now, swift!
Race with the golden sun!

ODE IN HER HONOR

When I converse with you quite peaceably,
I am enchanted you converse so peaceably.

When I dispute and voice all my reproaches,
Strange how you too dispute and offer me reproaches!

Alas, and should I be one mite unfaithful,
O misery! You scour the town to be unfaithful!

But if I should turn true for a short time,
Then you stay true to me but only for a time.

When I am happy you are happier
Still — and I happier to see you happier.

If I start weeping, then you weep beside me,
Should I be pressing, presto! there you are beside me!

When I swoon, then at once you too start swooning,
And I in turn swoon more when I behold you swooning.

Ah, tell me — when I die — will you die — you?
She: *Since I loved you best, I shall die more than you!*

. . . So I awakened from this dialogue:
It was only a dream (or what?) this dialogue.

NOCTURNE PARISIEN

Flow, dismal waters of the Seine; indolent, twist
Under your bridges lined with a nefarious mist . . .
How many corpses pass, gaunt, rotting without pity,
Whose hearts were crushed by you, inexorable city!
In your harsh icy waves no corpses you may find
To match the thoughts your aspect wakens in my mind!

Bright Tiber's banks are studded with vast ruins that show
Your traveler pomps and splendors faded long ago.
Covered with lichen and dark ivy, each ruin passes —
So many greyish heaps of stones amid green grasses . . .
The gay Guadalquivir smiles on blond orange trees,
Miming boleros and lithe fervent rhapsodies . . .
Pactolus flows with gold, Bosphorus offers shores
Where pale lascivious odalisks consort in sleepy scores . . .
The Rhine is like a baron and a troubadour
The delicate Lignon; a ruffian, the Adour . . .
The Nile's somnolent waters hold in plaintive keeping
Fond dreams with which to lull still mummies in their
        sleeping . . .
The Mississippi, proud of hallowed reeds, atwhiles
Augustly washes round its myriad bronzen isles,
And, flashing, sparks in an incredible display,
Crumbling in fierce Niagaras, splendent night and day . . .
Pallid Euphrates where swarms of familiar swans
Meld in white grace with virid tints a laurel dons,
And sing, rhythmic, caressing, as a poet sings,
Under clear skies streaked by eagle and vulture wings . . .
And, last, the Ganges, lined by tremulous high palm
On palm, and by red plainlands flows serene and calm

In royal train, while far away the noisy crowd
Moves past white temples, a live wave, howling to loud
Dense clicks of wooden cymbals — and while with thirsty
      throat,
Sustaining a prolonged and steady oboe note,
In wait till the deft antelope careens and bobs,
The yellow tiger stretches his striped back and sobs. . . .

But you, Seine, you have nothing! Just two quays, no more!
A filthy putrid quay spreading on either shore
With dreary musty books and idle crowds that squish
To spittle in the stream or catch unextant fish . . .

Yes, but when evening falls and strollers grow more rare,
Sleep-weighted, hunger-dulled, torpid with care,
When sunset burns red splotches in a sky that hums,
How blest for dreamers to emerge from dens in slums
And, elbowed on the Pont de la Cité, to stare
At Notre-Dame, dreaming in the cool peaceful air,
Hearts and hair windswept . . . Faint nocturnal breezes fly,
Russet and copper through a cool taciturn sky . . .
Over a king's head at a portal, slowly this
Last ray of a dead sun sets a vermilion kiss . . .
The swallow wings away at the approach of dark,
And you can watch the bat flutter, somber and stark . . .
Sounds fade and fade, all but a vague humming along
A far street proves the city lives to sing its song
Which licks its tyrants and which bites its prey betimes —
Now is the dawn of robbery, of loves and crimes.

Then suddenly — as a tenor — in a fierce wild despair,
Voicing his desperate cry against the darkening air
(A long cry of lament, shrill as a grim reminder)

From somewhere comes the medley of some organ grinder
Gurgling a polka or a ballad which we sung
Or thrummed on our harmonicas when we were young,
And which, lively or slow, joyous or gloomy, can
Explode in hearts of girl, artist or banished man . . .
Murdered, false-pitched, and would-be gay or
    melancholic,
Such tunes would give Rossini fever or the colic,
Such trailing laughs, such jagged plaints, such folderol
Roosting upon a crazed impervious key in *sol*
With rheumy wheezing notes and every *do* a *la*,
No matter, though, you weep in hearing them . . . And, ah!
The poet swept away to lands of radiant dreams
Feels these old chords send sap coursing through him in
    streams . . .
Pity wells up within his heart, tears fill his eyes,
His, now, the need of tasting peace in lofty skies,
As in a harmony, extraordinary and fantastic,
Which is at once a thing half-musical, half-plastic,
The soul floods all with its bright lyric benisons,
Mingling the organ notes with rays of setting suns.

The organ grinder vanishes. Now all is still.
Dull night sinks. Venus, rising on a distant hill,
Sways on a soft cloud where the dark of heaven falls,
Lamplighters spark the gaslamps on the city walls
And moon and gaslight zigzag unaccountably
In the Seine's waves, blacker than velvet masks can be.
The watcher by the railing of a *garde-fou*
Rusted by damp air, and years, like an ancient *sou*
Bends over the abyss, breathes its notes of perdition,
As thought, and hope serene, and high sublime ambition,

Everything, even memory, take fast to panic flight —
Himself left lonely with the Seine, Paris and Night.

Sinister trinity! Doors that brook no intrusions!
Mene, Tekel, Upharsin of our dead illusions!
You are such ghastly ghouls of evil and distress
That man, drunk with the pain your spectral fingers press
Deep through his flesh — wretched man who stands here
Orestes-like with never an Electra near,
Under the fatal magic of your hollow glance,
Leaps into the abyss to seek deliverance . . .
Your wicked trio is so jealous as it rides
Roughshod to kill and give the Worm his youngling brides
That none can tell which wreaks the maximum of blight,
Either to perish in you, Night, or in the fright
Of you, Seine, and the whirlpools your blind floods have
        swirled,
Or in your farded arms, Paris, queen of the world!

And still you flow, Seine, crawling ever without pity,
An agèd serpent fallowing across the city,
An agèd serpent bearing to far-distant havens
Cargoes of wood and coal and corpses and dead ravens. . . .

WOODLAND NOCTURNE

The trees tonight are heavy with distress,
Bowed down in contemplation of earth's grief,
Now never a wind, blowing in wantonness,
Shall clasp in his rough grasp a truant leaf
To brush against their bony nakedness.

Nothing can be more baleful than gaunt trees,
Sketched in harsh outline on the drape of night,
Like gnarled scarred hands that have wrought
    miseries,
But now, being powerless and without might,
Implore the aid of one who never sees.

Nothing can be more baleful than these are,
Most tragic penitents whose company
Renders them only lonelier by far:
Nothing is sadder than a naked tree
Against a sky too bleak to hold a star....

MANDOLINE

The serenaders in elation
And their fair listeners engage
In light insipid conversation
Under the lyric foliage.

Tircis and his Aminte are there
And there deathless Clitandre rehearses,
And Damis, who, for many a fair
Too cruel maid writes tender verses.

Their short silk jackets and the long
Trains of their trailing *robes à queue*
Their elegance, their joy, their song
And their blurred shadows, soft and blue,

Whirl in the vivid ecstasy
Of moons, part-rose, part grey; at ease,
The mandoline throbs aerily
Amid the tremors of the breeze.

CHARLEROI

In grasses black as ink
The Kobolds come and go,
The dense winds as they blow
Are weeping, you would think.

What feelings in this place?
The ears of wild oats whistle.
Bramble or gorse or thistle
Lashes the stroller's face.

Not houses here, instead
Hovels and huts; the eye
Traveling from sky to sky
Sees forges, fiery red.

What does one feel here? Ah,
The railway station thunders
The sight is lost in wonders
And where is Charleroi?

Sinister odors! Who
Or what is it we hear?
What hummed and rustled, clear
As ancient sistrums do?

Brutal sites for a set?
And oh, the breath, the eyes,
The flow of human sweat,
The harsh metallic cries!

In grasses black as ink
The Kobolds come and go,
The dense winds as they blow
Are weeping, you would think.

BRUSSELS MERRY-GO-ROUND

Whirl, whirl, good wooden steeds, whirl long and long,
Whirl five score times, whirl ten, whirl twenty score,
Whirl often, on and on, whirl evermore,
Whirl round and round to the blithe oboes' song.

The fat recruit and fatter housemaid play,
They ride your backs as snug as if in bed,
Long since the master and the mistress sped
To the Combre Woods to spend the holiday.

Whirl, horses of their hearts, turn round and round,
While, witness to your tournaments, the sly
Pickpocket blinks a scrutinizing eye —
Whirl, whirl to the triumphant piston's play.

Delightful how it makes you drunk to stroll
Through this fool circus, semi-gay, half-sad!
How good your belly feels, your head how bad! —
Bad by the shovelful, good by the shoal . . .

Whirl round, whirl round and never know the need
For using spurs in future or instanter
To prick your gallant mounts into a canter,
Whirl round and round with never hope of feed.

Haste, horses of their souls, since time and tide
Ebb as the darkening shadows fall; the dove
Now seeks her pigeon for the rites of love,
Far from the Fair and far from Madame's side.

Whirl round, whirl round, turn as the black night comes.
Lover and mistress now depart. Behold:
Slowly the velvet sky dons stars of gold:
Whirl round and round to the brisk roll of drums. . . .

36

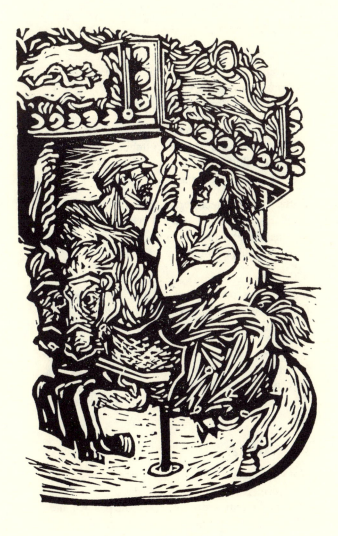

PROMENADE

How pallid is the sky, how frail the trees . . .
They smile on our gay costumes as these flare
Trippingly on light breezes with an air
Of nonchalance and wings fluttering at ease.

A soft wind wrinkles the small fount. A fine
Last ray of sunshine breaks, attenuated
By the low lindens of the lane. Abated,
It sinks bluish, perishing by design.

Blithe schooled deceiver and charming coquette,
Tenderest hearts, yet pledged to no stern vow,
We chat delightfully and anyhow
What marquis would not tease an amoret?

The ladies have an unwatched hand that knows
Skilled ways to slap a face. The redness lingers,
Quits to be pardoned if you kiss their fingers,
Mostly the little one . . . And so it goes . . .

Excessive, light, your punishment the drouth
Of an indifferent glance, exceeding dry!
Placed in sharp contrast, howsoever, by
The somewhat clement pout of the soft mouth!

ANGUISH

Not your nourishsome fields . . . nor echoes,
      vermeil-bright,
Of your Sicilian pastorals . . . nor the pale witchery
Of your auroral pomp . . . nor the solemnity

Of dolent suns that die under the spell of night,
Move me, Nature.... I laugh at Art and mankind's plight,
At song, at verse, Greek temples, belfries spirally
Soaring from churches through void skies in twisted glee;
I jest at good or bad, I mock both wrong and right....

I bear no faith in God, I abjure and deny
All thought whatever; as for that old irony
Called Love, it is a lie which I shall not abide....
Weary of living and afraid of death, I ail,
My soul like a small brig, the toy of any tide,
Sails trimmed for hideous shipwreck in the gale.

TO A WOMAN

For you this verse because of the consoling grace
Of your wide eyes in which reveries laugh and weep,
Because your heart is pure and good, this verse to keep,
Made of my fierce distress and violent disgrace....
Alas! what hideous nightmares haunt my soul to trace
Harvests of mad and jealous furies I must reap,
Multiplied as a pack of starving wolves.... How steep
My road, how gaunt my heart, a rent and bloodied place!

Atrociously I suffer under sorrow's sign,
So that the first lament of the first sinner banished
From Eden is a blithesome eclogue next to mine!...
What paltry cares you may have known are swiftly
        vanished,
Like swallows winging on autumnal skies — remember,
Darling? — across cool afternoons in late September!

39

THE NIGHTINGALE

Like a shrill flight of crazed birds overhead,
My memories swoop down, disquieted,
Swoop down on my heart's yellow leaves to stare
At its bent alder-trunk reflected there
In the blue tinfoil waters of Regret
That flow by, melancholy. Jet by jet
They swoop down; then the evil clamors cease
As a cool breeze rises to bring them peace
While they die slowly in the tree until
After a moment everything is still.
Silence — save for the rapt accents that sing
The Absent One! — accents how languishing
Trilled by that bird, my first love, whose soft rhymes
Make music as in those first far-off times . . .
Now in the moonlight's sad relucent play,
In all solemnity and pallor, a
Melancholy and summer-weighted night
Falls, fraught with silence, black and infinite,
And in the blue, which a blithe breeze has stirred,
Cradles the quivering tree and weeping bird.

NEVERMORE

Oh, memory, memory . . . What would you have? . . .
    Autumn's moan
Sent the thrush flying across an air free of all tone,
As the sun darted one sad ray in monotone
On yellowing woods where the raw breezes howl and
    groan.

40

Dreaming our dreams, in company we sped,
Just she and I; winds fanned our thought and head,
Sudden, she turned to me; her glance was garlanded:
"What was your happiest day?" her aureate voice said,

Her sweet sonorous voice, in cool angelic pitch . . .
For answer I but smiled discreetly, after which
I kissed her tenuous white hand religiously.
Ah, fragrances of the first flowers we discover!
And what a talismanic charm in the first *Oui*
That flutters on the lips of a young lover.

VOTIVE OFFERING

Oarystis!* Meetings that your first sweethearts bless!
The gold of hair, the blue of eyes, the flower of flesh,
And in the scent of bodies, young and fresh,
The craintive spontaneity of each caress.
How far they are, these moments of stark happiness,
And all that purity! How my darksome winters press,
Trapped in the springtime of regret as in a mesh —
Winters of my ennui, repugnance and distress. . . .

So here I am now, dismal, lonely and alone,
Dismal and desperate, cold as a stone,
An orphan with no older sister to bear aid —
No woman with your glowing love, tender and mild,
Gentle and pensive, unsurprised and unafraid,
Kissing my brow, as who might kiss a child. . . .

* A Greek noun founded on a verb meaning "To live in
tender intimacy."

41

GREEN

Here fruit and flower, here branch and leaf in strands,
And here my heart, which beats for you alone,
Forbear from rending it with white lithe hands:
A humble gift — but make of it your own!

I come covered with dew which, sharp as sleet,
The morning wind froze on my fervent brow;
Suffer my weariness, prone at your feet,
To dream of solace you shall grant it now.

Let your young breasts lull my tired head, still warm,
Still throbbing with your kiss, the last and best,
Let it find peace after the happy storm,
So let me slumber since you lie at rest!

SPLEEN

The roses were of deepest red,
The ivy vines of deepest black —
Darling, you need but turn your head
And all my hopelessness comes back.

Too tender was the sky, too blue!
Too green the sea, the air too light . . .
I always fear — to wait spells rue! —
Lest you take to atrocious flight.

I tire of velvet holly trees,
Of boxtrees bright as burnished brass,
Of all the land's immensities,
And of all things save you, alas!

STREETS

Let's dance a jig!

Chiefly I loved her shining eyes,
Brighter than stars in limpid skies,
Malicious, too, and very wise —
Let's dance a jig!

Truly she knew strange ways of harming
A luckless lover; his alarming
Melancholy proved wholly charming —
Let's dance a jig!

But now, since she's stone-dead to me,
Her flowerlike kisses seem to be
Her most exquisite quality —
Let's dance a jig!

And I recall and I recall
The times and words we spoke, and all
The best of things that could befall —
Let's dance a jig!

O TRISTE, TRISTE...

Sad, sad my soul in its sad rueing,
It was, it was a woman's doing.

I found no solace elsewhere though
My heart went hence where it should go

And though my soul, and though my heart
Fled from this woman's evil art,

43

I found no solace elsewhere though
My heart went hence where it should go.

My heart, fashioned too tenderly
Asked of my soul: *"Can such things be?*

"Can such things be? Did they take place
This sad proud exile and disgrace?"

My soul answered my heart: *"Do I*
Myself know what these snares imply:

"I, being present although banished,
Although gone hence long since and vanished."

LANGUOR

I am the Empire in its final decadence,
Watching tall white Barbarians filing slowly by,
As I compose languid acrostics which must lie
Couched in gold style under the hot sun's somnolence.
My lonely soul sickens. Its boredom is too dense.
Yonder, they say, long warfare drills a flaming sky,
I am too feeble to face warfare and too shy
To storm a world of force too sharp and too intense.

Since I have neither strength nor will, let me expire . . .
The dregs are long since drained. Bathyllus, stay your
    laughter!
All is eaten and quaffed, and there is no word after . . .
Only some trifling verses fit to feed a fire,
Only a playboy slave, dooming me to neglect,
Only ennui, the source of which none shall detect.

44

PERPLEXITY

I can never know why
My mind so bitterly
Flutters with mad and tireless pinions over the sea . . .

Over all dear to me
My love with frightened, shy
Wing broods, skimming the water's surface. Why, oh why?

A sea-gull in sorrowful flight,
My thought follows the wave and sways
At every wind in the skyways
And, with the tide, veers left or right —
A sea-gull in sorrowful flight.

Drunk with sunlight and wild
With rapture, being free,
An instinct guides it over this immensity.
The breezes, summery
And blithe and mild,
Bear it in a half-sleep, comforted and beguiled.

Sometimes so melancholy its crying
That pilots flinch at its dire notes,
Then it yields to the winds, and floats
And plunges, and soars heavenward, flying
Again, and so melancholy its crying!

I can never know why
My mind so bitterly
Flutters with mad and tireless wing over the sea . . .

Over all dear to me
My love with frightened, shy
Wing broods, skimming the water's surface. Why, oh why?

WEEPING HEART

Tears reign in my heart
As it rains on the town,
What languorous smart
Now harrows my heart?

O the lilt of the rain
On green earth and grey roofs,
For a heart bored and vain,
O the lilt of the rain!

Tears reign without reason,
Striking this stricken heart.
What? No semblance of treason,
Yet grief without reason!

What more sorrowful fate
Than not quite knowing why,
Shorn of love and of hate,
Grief and woe are my fate!

LA-BAS

The sky spreads over the far roof
 So blue, so calm,
As a tree over the far roof
 Sways like a palm.

The bell there in the sky we see
 Is tinkling faint,
A bird perched on the tree we see
 Chants in complaint.

Ah God, ah God! all life is there,
    Plain as a ditty!
The peaceful echoes we hear there
    Come from the city.

What have you made, you I behold
    (O endless tears!)
Speak, what was made, you I behold,
    Of your best years?

OF HER NAME

A saint with her bright aureole,
A chatelaine in her high tower,
All that the words of human soul
Contain in grace and love and power,

The golden notes that horns express
Through the far woods in answering rhymes,
Wedded to the proud tenderness
Of noble Dames in ancient times,

With these, the signal charm stamped on
Cool smiles victoriously smiled,
Echoes of whiteness of the swan,
Of peach-red in the woman-child,

Aspects of pearl and white and pink,
Patrician greetings, kindly fame —
I see and hear all these, I think,
In her sweet Carolingian name.

47

LIMPING SONNET

No, this end is too grim! No, this is truly *triste!*
No man should be allowed to suffer such mischance.
No, truly this is like the death of a dumb beast
Who sees his life blood ebb under his withered glance.
London Town smokes and screams. Cursed city of the
    Bible!
The gaslight flames and floats, the signs are crimson rags,
The mean houses contract, their shriveling is frightful,
As terrifying as a senate of frail hags.

The whole grim past leaps up to whine, to mew, to yelp
Across the filthy red-and-yellow fog of Sohos
With echoed *yesses, ays, indeeds, all rights* and *ohos!*
No, his is martyrdom beyond all hope of help.
No, this end is too grim, too truly *triste*, too frightful,
And oh! Heaven's fire above this city of the Bible!

LONDON

The din of pubs . . . the muck of filthy pavements where
Decaying plane trees shed their leaves in the dark air . . .
The bus, a hurricane of ironware and mud,
Ill-set between its wheels . . . its screech, its roar, its thud,
Its green-and-red eyes goggling slowly . . . Workmen going
Off to their clubs, the stale puffs of their stinkpipes
    blowing
Into the coppers' eyes . . . roofs leaking ceaselessly . . .
Walls oozing dampness . . . streams gushing torrentially
Down gutters . . . broken asphalt, slippery as ice:
There lies my road, and at its end lies Paradise.

48

EVENING'S END

The hearth and the lamp's narrow strand of light . . .
You sit, finger to temple, dreams glow bright,
Your every look lost in the loved one's looks,
The hour of steaming tea and of closed books,
The joy to feel that evening is abating,
The charming weariness and blissful waiting
For nuptial shadows and for kindly night . . .
My tenderest dreams pursue this with delight
And ceaselessly across all vain delays,
Febrile at months and weeks, furious at days!

THE MASKED HORSEMAN

Gallant masked cavalier who rides in silent trance,
Long since misfortune pierced my heart with its sharp
    lance.

Veins of my agèd heart bled one red jet — just one —
Then died under the lustrous flowers and pale sun.

The shadows blinded me. A cry rose to my lips
As my old heart died in a tremulous eclipse.

Then Lord Misfortune reined his charger very near,
Then he dismounted and his chill hand touched me here!

His iron-gauntled finger pressed deep through my wound,
He read his harsh law harshly; as, amazed, I swooned.

At the cold contact of his iron hand, I bowed,
While a new heart was born within me, pure and proud,

And thus, in all-divine purity, ever blest,
I felt a new young gentle heart born in my breast.

I stood there trembling, drunk, incredulous and odd
As any man who glimpses visions of his God.

Then the true knight leaped on his horse again and sped
Far far away, but vanishing, he bowed his head

And cried — (I can still hear him!) — in tones cold as rime,
Leastways, be careful, lad. This is the long last time.

DEAD

The dead that you have bled in the grave's pall
    Are always well-avenged, God knows!
They have their ways, and pity those who fall
    Under the curse that overthrows . . .
Better not to have known life or drawn breath,
Better slow death followed by slower death,
For Time is long, and harsh its muffled blows.

The living that you hurt and make to bleed
    Sometimes seek vengeance, young or old,
And those they seize are pitiful indeed
    Caught in avengement's stranglehold . . .
Better a bear's sharp brutal paw at that,
Better the hempen rope for a cravat,
Better Othello's bolster, manifold!

You, persecutor, fear the vampire's curse
    And fear the vicious strangler too,
The day of wrath shall dawn, fiercer and worse
    Than ever grief or pain or rue,
Surprising the assassin as a crime
And pouncing on the theft as robbers do!

PRISON SKETCH

Lady Mouse scurries
Black in the dusk's grey light,
Lady Mouse scurries
Grey in the jet-black night.

The bell tolls its warning:
Good prisoners, slumber deep!
The bell tolls its warning,
You really *must* sleep!

No bad nightmares now,
Dream of but your amours,
No bad nightmares now,
Dream of belles and their lures.

The moon is shining full,
Sleepers snore loudly here,
The moon is shining full,
Actual and clear.

A cloud drifts trailing over,
All is black as blackest doom,
A cloud drifts trailing over,
Look! Day breaks the gloom.

Lady Mouse scurries
Rose in blue daylight tones,
Lady Mouse scurries,
Get up, lazybones!

PARABLES

Bless Thee, Lord, who did make a Christian out of *me*
In these times when fierce ignorance and hatred reign,
Yet grant me power and placid courage to remain
Always as true and faithful as a dog to Thee,
To be the destined lamb whose steps obediently
Follow his mother and bring the shepherd boy no pain,
Feeling that beyond wool he owes his life again
And ever to his Lord for such felicity.

Grant that I be the fish, a cypher for the Son,
The obscure ass He rode once in triumphant bliss,
And in my flesh the swine He drove to the abyss,
For beasts, better than men or women, blithely run
(In these times of rebellion and duplicity)
To do their humble duty with simplicity.

THE SHELLS

In the grotto where amorously
We lay, each shell incrusted bears
Its own particularity.
One, crimson like our twin souls, shares
The glow of our hearts' blood which flares
When I burn and you burn likewise. . . .
One, which affects your languor, lies
Pale as you rest, with, on your face,
Umbrage against my mocking eyes. . . .
Another counterfeits the grace
Of your pink ear and, fleck for fleck,
One matches your short rosy neck.

(But one, among the others, disturbs me strangely!)

54

SERENADE

Even as a dead man's song in a lost hour,
From a dead man's ditch,
Hark, mistress, as my voice soars to your bower,
Raucous, shrill, off-pitch.

Open your heart and hearing to the blessing
That my strings intone,
I made my song at once cruel and caressing
For yourself alone.

Your gold and onyx both shall be my text,
Where no shadow rests,
The Styx of your black hair, the Lethe next
Of your tranquil breasts.

Even as a dead man's song in a lost hour
From a dead man's ditch,
Hark, mistress, as my voice soars to your bower,
Raucous, shrill, off-pitch.

Next, I shall magnify your blessed flesh
In worshipful rite,
And next, its lavish savors which refresh
Night on sleepless night.

Concluding, I shall sing the crimson vise
Of your lips and more
Your skilled sweet ways to wrack and martyrize,
O Angel, O Whore!

Open your heart and hearing to the blessing
That my strings intone:
I made my song at once cruel and caressing
For yourself alone!

WENCH

An ugly Boucher model, she,
But without powder in her hair.
Gloriously blond, her witching air
Tempts all men to debauchery.

But she is chiefly mine, I know —
That mane my kisses overlaid,
That small and fiery cascade
Which burns my blood from top to toe!

Ay, mine the more, without surcease,
That precinct, dazzling and ornate,
That lies around the holy gate:
That gold, divine, fostering fleece!

And who could sing this body whole,
Save me, its worshiper and priest,
Meek slave and master at a feast
For which he blithely damns his soul?

Her loved rare flesh, harmonious, lies
Suave, white as the white rose is white,
White as pure milk and rosy-bright
As lilies under crimson skies.

Proud thighs, sharp teats the bosom tenses,
Back, belly and loins at the behest
Of eyes and hands avid in quest
Of the parched lips, of all the senses!

Sweet let us see if still the red
Curtain is drawn over the pillow
Which soars and sways, a magic billow
On the wild sheets . . . To bed, to bed!

TEDIUM

In the unending and
Dead stretch of the plain
Uncertain snows shine vain
As sheets of twinkling sand.

Copperish hangs the sky
With never a glow or gleam
You would believe your dream
Sees the moon live and die.

In the woods over there
The oaks are clouds that swim
Greyly across the dim
Vaporous humid air.

Copperish hangs the sky
With never a glow or gleam,
You would believe your dream
Sees the moon live and die.

O broken-winded crows,
And you, wolves, famine-thinned,
In this harsh winter wind,
How merciless your woes!

In the unending and
Dead stretch of the plain
Uncertain snows shine vain
As sheets of twinkling sand.

KYRIE ELEISON

Pity, O Lord, our misery,
Christ, pity our distress,

Grant us honor and victory
Make our foe powerless,
Pity, O Lord, our misery.

Increase our faith and gentleness
Far from Sin's witchery,
Christ, pity our distress.

Sift us, as winnowers, jealously
Sift the grain they possess,
Pity, O Lord, our misery.

Through faith vouchsafe us happiness,
This we implore on bended knee,
Christ, pity our distress.

This we implore on bended knee,
Through love, vouchsafe us happiness,
Pity, O Lord, our misery.

Through hope, Lord, grant felicity,
Christ, dower us with happiness,
Christ, pity our distress,

Pity, O Lord, our misery.

SAGESSE

O Lord God, Thou hast wounded me with love
And the wound deep within me is throbbing still,
O Lord God, Thou hast wounded me with love.

O Lord God, fear of Thee has stricken me
Now the burn is still there throbbing within me,
O Lord God, fear of Thee has stricken me.

O Lord God, I have known all that is vile,
Yet has Thy glory made its house in me,
O Lord God, I have known all that is vile.

Immerse my soul in waves of Thy good Wine,
Meld my life with the good Bread of Thy table,
Immerse my soul in waves of Thy good Wine.

Here is my blood which I have never spilled,
Here is my flesh unworthy to be bruised,
Here is my blood which I have never spilled.

Here is my brow that could do naught but blush
Set as a soul for Thy thrice-hallowed feet,
Here is my brow that could do naught but blush.

Here are my hands which wrought not any labor
For the censer's live coals and for rare incense,
Here are my hands which wrought not any labor.

Here is my heart which beats only in vain
To throb under the thorns of Calvary,
Here is my heart which beats only in vain.

Here are my feet, frivolous voyagers
To hasten at the first cry of Thy grace,
Here are my feet, frivolous voyagers.

Here is my voice, a sullen lying rumor
For the deserved rebukes of Penitence,
Here is my voice, a sullen lying rumor.

Here are my eyes, luminaries of error
To be extinguished in the tears of prayer,
Here are my eyes, luminaries of error.

Alas! Thou, God of offering and pardon,
Knowest the wells of my ingratitude,
Alas! Thou, God of offering and pardon

Thou, God of terror, God of sanctity,
Knowest alas! the black pit of my crime,
Thou, God of terror, God of sanctity,

Thou, God of Peace, of joy, of happiness,
Thou knowest all my fears and ignorance,
Thou, God of peace, of joy, of happiness,

Thou knowest all this, O God, all this, all this,
And how I am the poorest of all men,
Thou knowest all this, O God, all this, all this,
But what I have, O God, I give to Thee.